Angélica
Dass

THE
COLORS
WE
SHARE

aperture

You may have heard skin color described as "black," "white," "red," or "yellow." But have you ever met a person who is actually one of these colors?

Of course you haven't!
No one's skin is really one
of those colors—not a
single person in the entire
world, including you.

Humans are much
more colorful!

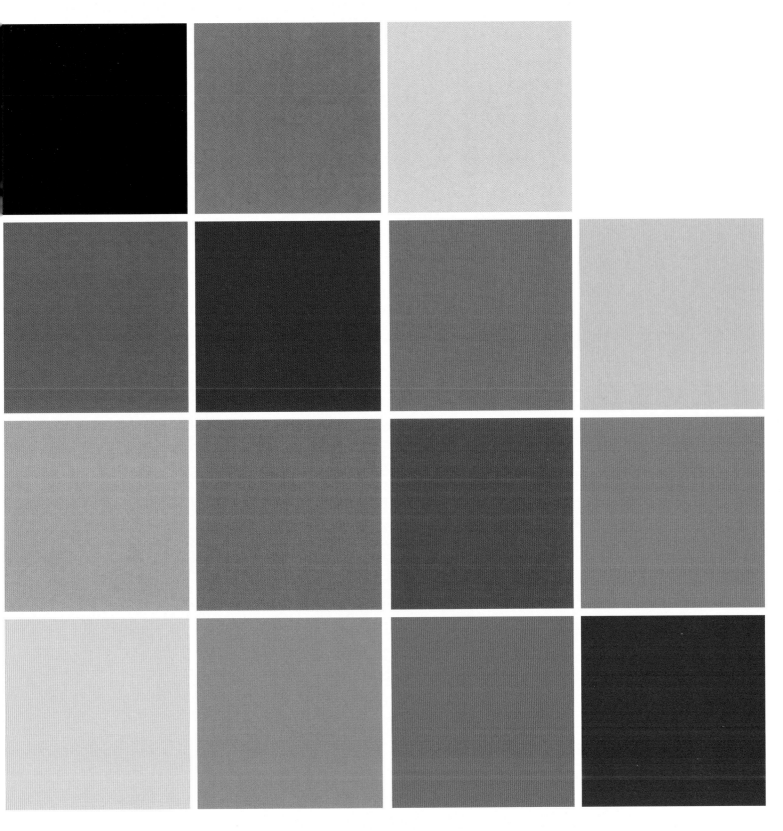

Yet the way we live today, people are divided into "races" based on those colors and are treated differently because of these groupings.

This thinking is too small
for a world that contains
so many beautiful colors
and people.

It is as wrong as thinking
that the world is flat!

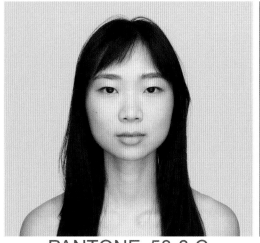

PANTONE® 58-8 C

PANTONE® 322-1 C

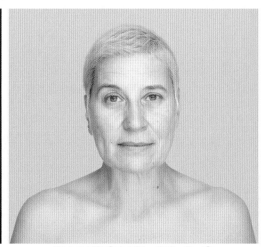

PANTONE® 92-9 C

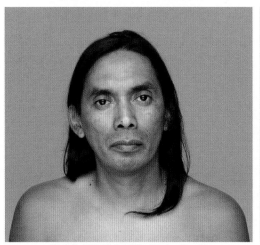

PANTONE® 71-5 C

PANTONE® 62-8 C

PANTONE® 72-5 C

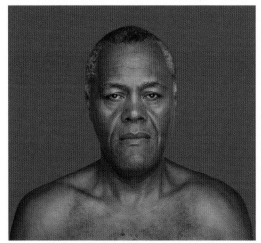

PANTONE® 317-5 C

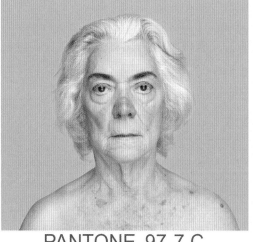

PANTONE® 97-7 C

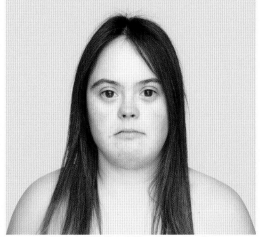

PANTONE® 51-8 C

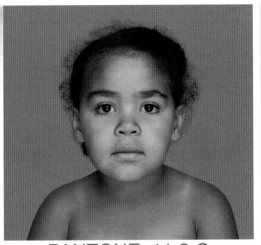

PANTONE® 44-2 C

PANTONE® 99-9 C

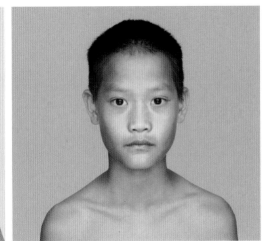

PANTONE® 51-5 C

PANTONE® 51-6 C

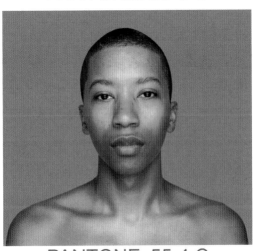

PANTONE® 55-4 C

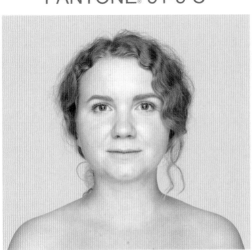

PANTONE® 77-8 C

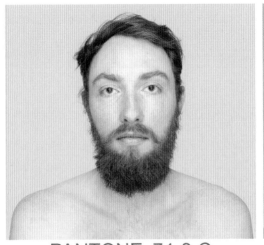

PANTONE® 74-8 C

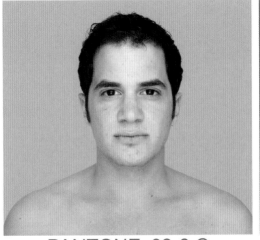

PANTONE® 62-6 C

PANTONE® 45-3 C

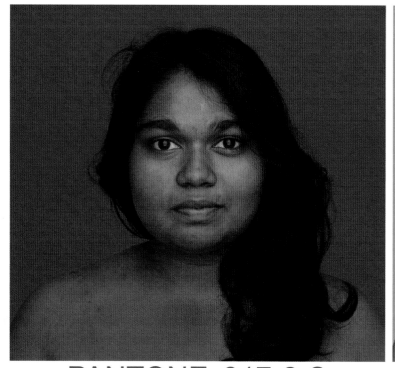

PANTONE® 317-2 C

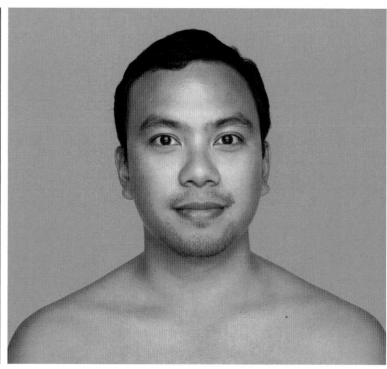

PANTONE® 62-5 C

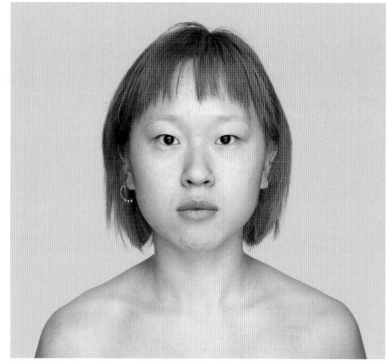

PANTONE® 58-8 C

PANTONE® 116-5 C

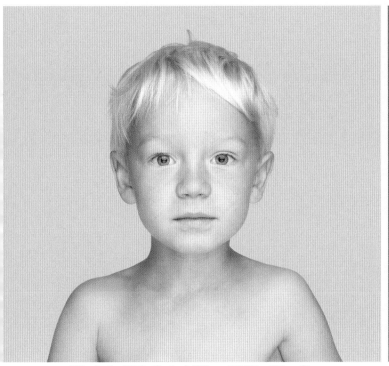

PANTONE® 57-7 C

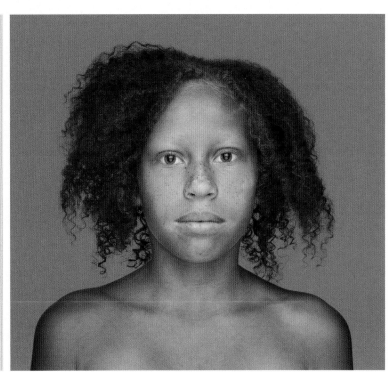

PANTONE® 54-9 C

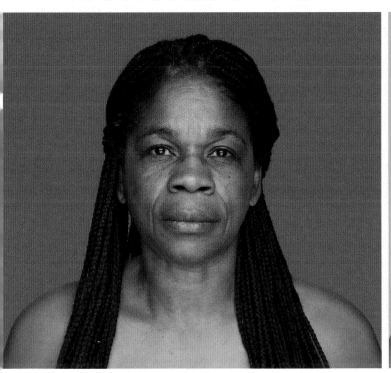

PANTONE® 59-3 C

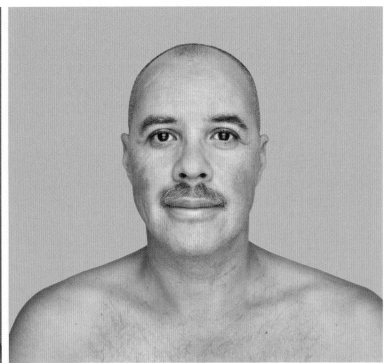

PANTONE® 75-7 C

PANTONE® 322-1 C

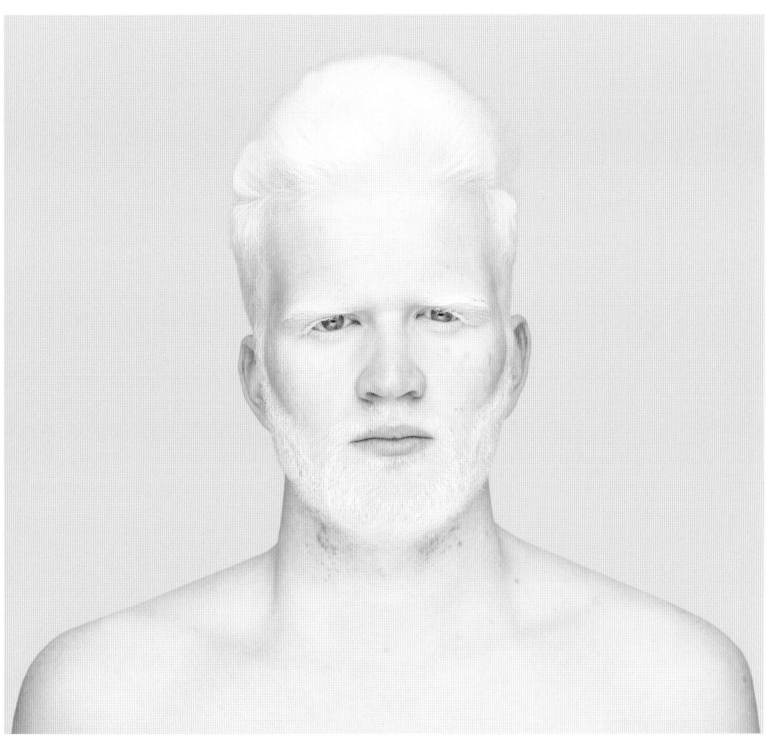

PANTONE® 75-9 C

Even though it seems like
we're talking about color,
we're really talking about
how we see each other,

and what we believe
about others based on
the color of their skin.

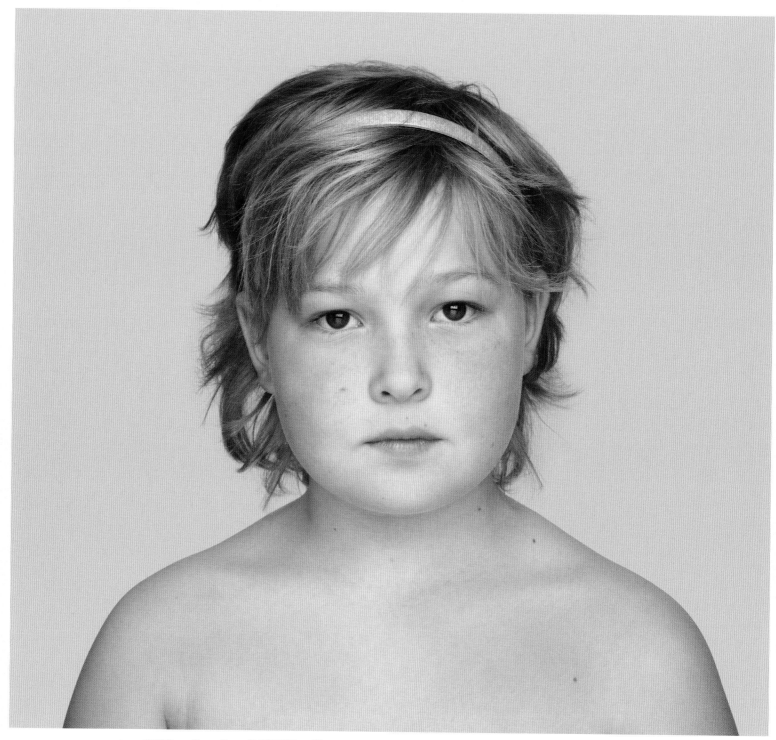

PANTONE® 58-7 C

PANTONE® 58-7 C

You might be surprised to
see that these four people,
who could all be labeled
different "races," have the
same color skin!

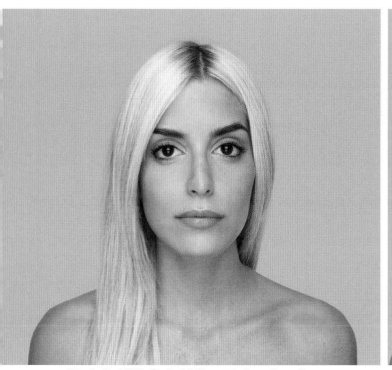

PANTONE® 58-6 C

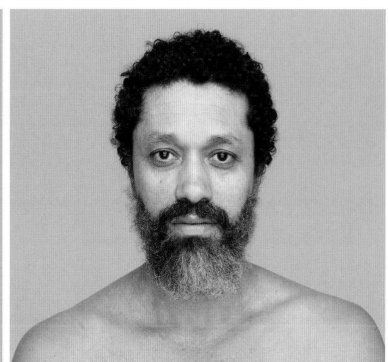

PANTONE® 58-6 C

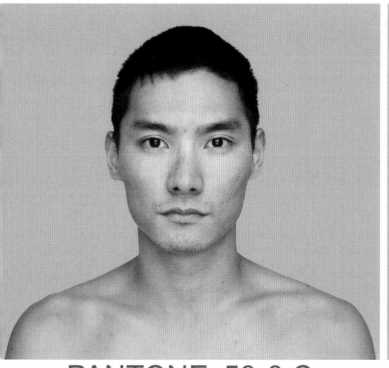

PANTONE® 58-6 C

PANTONE® 58-6 C

PANTONE® 66-3 C

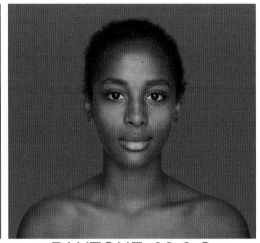

PANTONE® 66-3 C

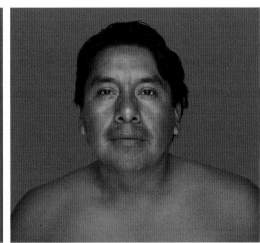

PANTONE® 66-3 C

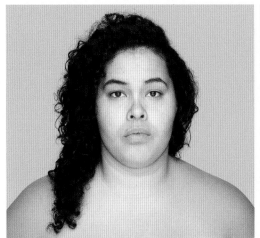

PANTONE® 53-7 C

PANTONE® 53-7 C

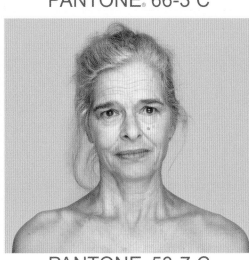

PANTONE® 53-7 C

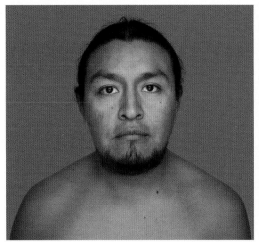

PANTONE® 66-5 C

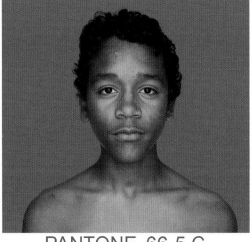

PANTONE® 66-5 C

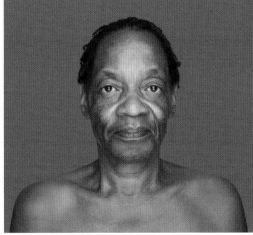

PANTONE® 66-5 C

Every person is unique, even if
they share the same skin color.

To know a person's story, you
need to get to know them.

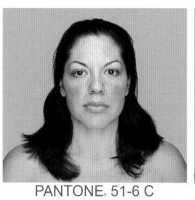

PANTONE 51-6 C

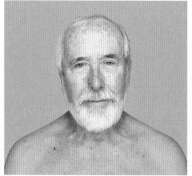

PANTONE 98-7 C

PANTONE 4625 C

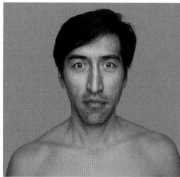

PANTONE 59-5 C

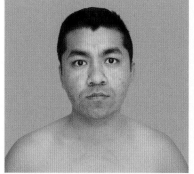

PANTONE 58-5 C

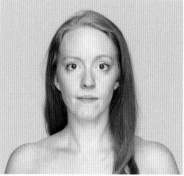

PANTONE 94-8 C

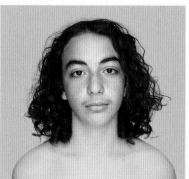

PANTONE 50-6 C

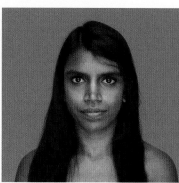

PANTONE 59-4 C

PANTONE 323-1 C

PANTONE 54-7 C

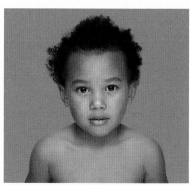

PANTONE 59-5 C

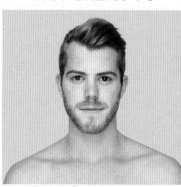

PANTONE 108-8 C

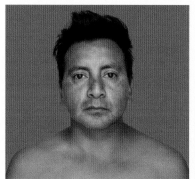

PANTONE 64-4 C

PANTONE 74-7 C

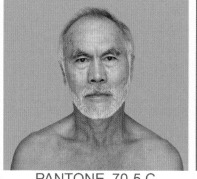

PANTONE 70-5 C

PANTONE 316-6 C

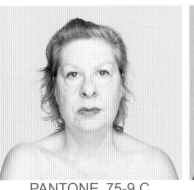

PANTONE 75-9 C

PANTONE 77-7 C

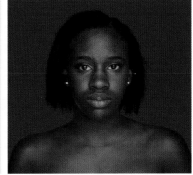

PANTONE 320-2 C

PANTONE 78-6 C

PANTONE 321-2 C

PANTONE 63-6 C

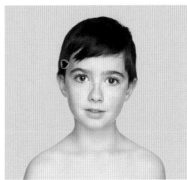

PANTONE 92-9 C

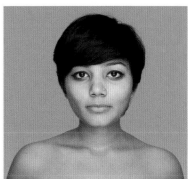

PANTONE 52-5 C

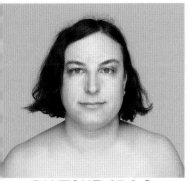

PANTONE 67-6 C

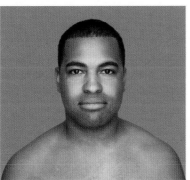

PANTONE 55-4 C

PANTONE 62-8 C

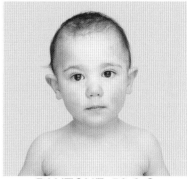

PANTONE 58-8 C

PANTONE 80-6 C

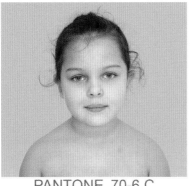

PANTONE 70-6 C

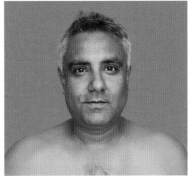

PANTONE 64-5 C

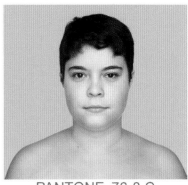

PANTONE 76-8 C

Your story is unique, but do you know how similar you are to others too?

Even with our differences, humans are 99.9% biologically identical!

Only in that last, tiny 0.1% do you find skin, hair, and eye color. Grouping people by skin color is not scientific at all.

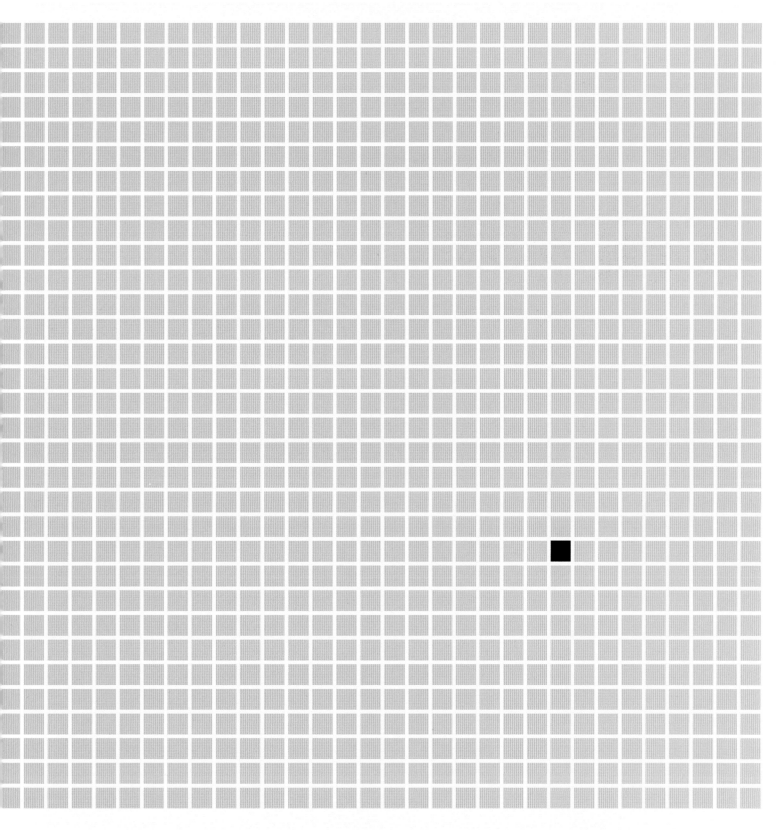

You have your own special skin color, and it's not just one color, but a combination, like a painter mixes with paints.

From the three primary colors—blue, red, and yellow—along with black and white, you can create a universe of colors, including the color of everyone you know!

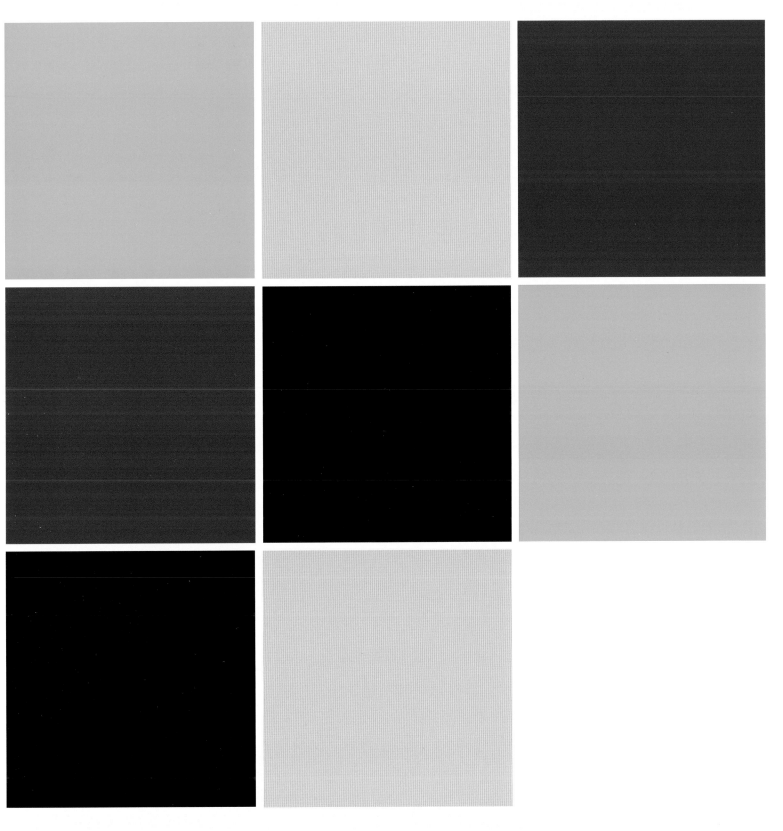

To find your color with paint,
mix yellow and blue to make
green, then add in red to create
brown—because melanin, the
pigment that gives all human
skin its color, is brown.

Now look in a mirror. Add black
and white to better match your
skin tone. Then try adding a
little bit more yellow and red to
see if you can get even closer.

These are the colors we share!

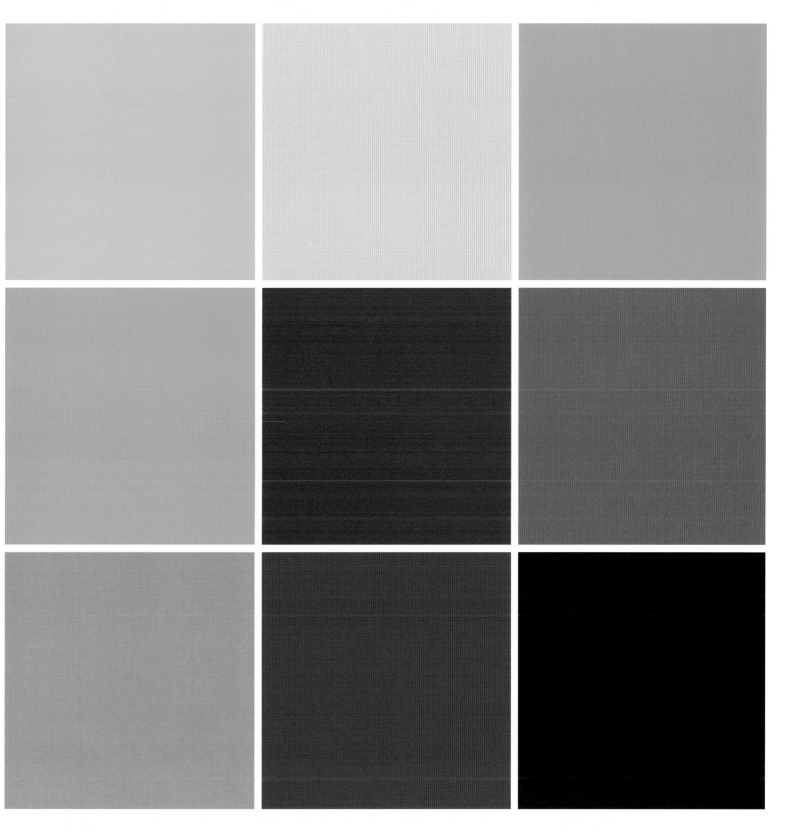

PANTONE₆ 1545 C

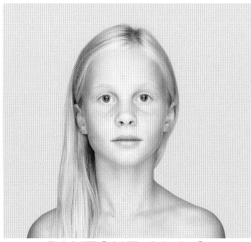

PANTONE₆ 38-8 C

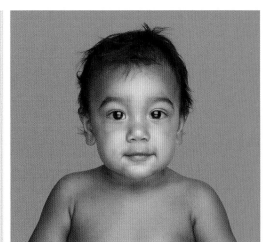

PANTONE₆ 59-5 C

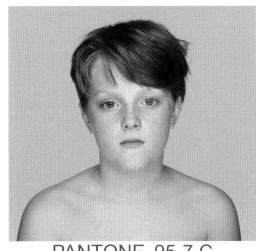

PANTONE₆ 95-7 C

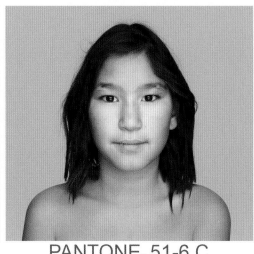

PANTONE₆ 51-6 C

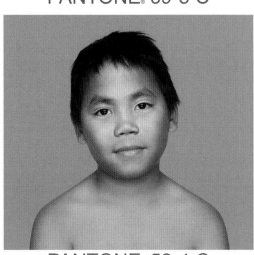

PANTONE₆ 58-4 C

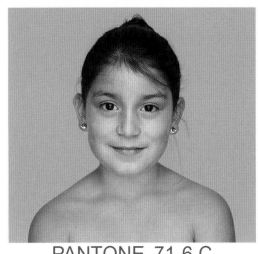

PANTONE₆ 71-6 C

PANTONE₆ 75-9 C

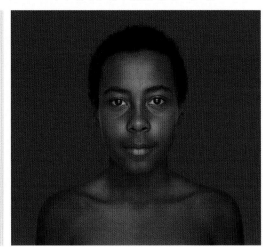

PANTONE₆ 320-2 C

We are made from the
same ingredients, and
yet each of us is uniquely
different. This is the
beauty of being human.

PANTONE. 59-3 C

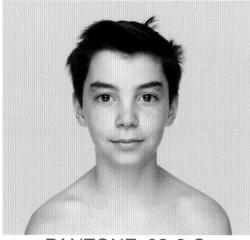

PANTONE. 62-8 C

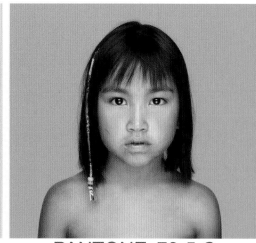

PANTONE. 70-5 C

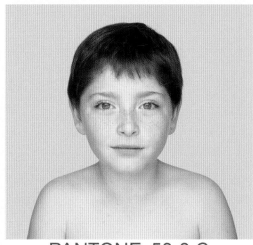

PANTONE. 58-8 C

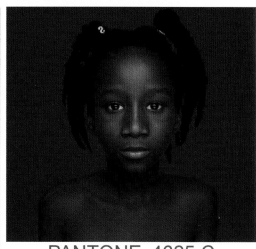

PANTONE. 4625 C

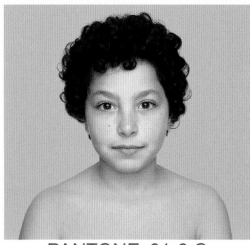

PANTONE. 61-6 C

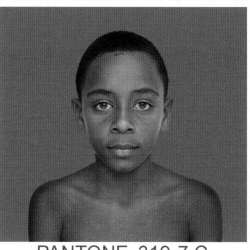

PANTONE. 319-7 C

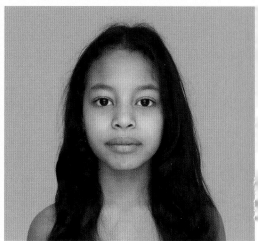

PANTONE. 51-5 C

We all have something
different to offer.
And so our differences
do not need to divide us!

Together we can question
old ideas and think bigger...

PANTONE. 321-2 C   PANTONE. 88-9 C   PANTONE. 62-9 C   PANTONE. 67-5 C   PANTONE. 54-7 C

PANTONE. 51-5 C   PANTONE. 57-6 C   PANTONE. 59-4 C   PANTONE. 51-8 C   PANTONE. 60-5 C

PANTONE. 59-4 C   PANTONE. 75-8 C   PANTONE. 71-7 C   PANTONE. 317-6 C   PANTONE. 331-8 C

PANTONE. 81-6 C   PANTONE. 319-2 C   PANTONE. 61-5 C   PANTONE. 62-6 C   PANTONE. 75-7 C

PANTONE. 317-2 C   PANTONE. 75-6 C   PANTONE. 74-8 C   PANTONE. 66-5 C   PANTONE. 57-7 C

PANTONE 318-3 C   PANTONE 35-11 C   PANTONE 316-6 C   PANTONE 63-9 C   PANTONE 68-5 C

PANTONE 78-8 C   PANTONE 80-7 C   PANTONE 58-5 C   PANTONE 320-2 C   PANTONE 67-6 C

PANTONE 322-1 C   PANTONE 52-4 C   PANTONE 91-8 C   PANTONE 70-6 C   PANTONE 62-5 C

PANTONE 65-5 C   PANTONE 95-7 C   PANTONE 80-6 C   PANTONE 64-7 C   PANTONE 317-3 C

PANTONE 44-3 C   PANTONE 59-5 C   PANTONE 92-9 C   PANTONE 68-4 C   PANTONE 321-6 C

ACKNOWLEDGMENTS

To my ancestors for their guidance.

My grandmothers Kilda, Sebastiana, and Aracy for shaping my character.

My colorful family.

Rafa Fenoy for his faith in me.

Elaine and Ben.

Marian Leon, Mercedes Cosano, Alex Mena, Wendy Espinal, and Nuria Cubas for being part of this journey.

The entire TED community, especially the translators and my TED RES 5 family.

The whole Aperture team, particularly Denise Wolff and Lanah Swindle, for accompanying me toward this big goal and bringing me light during the pandemic.

Elaine Ramos and Flávia Castanheira who, through this design, materialized my dream.

Educators and teachers around the world who choose to make a difference.

Each of you who sat in front of my camera and who build this Humanae family.

All who share and amplify Humanae's message.

Thank you for so much love, which is fuel for me (and us) to continue.

Angélica Dass

ABOUT THIS BOOK

For the portraits in this book, the artist Angélica Dass photographed each person and then carefully matched the background to the skin color of their nose! She selects the background from a giant color palette called Pantone and includes the color code—the word *Pantone* followed by a series of numbers and letters—below the picture each time. (By the way, the purply blue used throughout the book is called Pantone 072C.) By using this technical language instead of the words we often use to describe skin color, she helps us see how wonderfully colorful humans really are and think about the concept of race in a new way.

And, in case you've been wondering, the people in these portraits are wearing clothes (just outside of the camera frame)!

ABOUT THE AUTHOR

Angélica Dass is a Brazilian artist of African, European, and Native American descent who lives in Spain. She was happy growing up in a family full of colors. Outside her home, however, things were different. Her skin color had many other meanings: "I remember my first art classes were exciting, but I never understood that one 'flesh'-colored pencil," she says. "I was made of flesh, but I'm not pink. My skin is brown, yet people said I was black. I had a mess of colors in my head." Inspired by her family tree, she created the Humanae project to question the concept of race and show that skin color is much more complex than the categories we use. The project now includes over 4,500 portraits of volunteers from all over the world and is still ongoing, inviting us all to reflect on how we see each other and ourselves.

THE COLORS WE SHARE
by Angélica Dass

Cover images: Angélica Dass

Editor: Denise Wolff
Editorial Assistant: Lanah Swindle
Designers: Elaine Ramos & Flávia Castanheira
Senior Production Manager: True Sims
Production Manager: Andrea Chlad
Senior Text Editor: Susan Ciccotti
Copy Editors: Alexa Dilworth, Elena Goukassian
Work Scholar: Joanna Knutsen

Additional staff of the Aperture book program includes:
Chris Boot, Executive Director; Lesley A. Martin, Creative
Director; Taia Kwinter, Publishing Manager; Emily Patten,
Publishing Assistant; Samantha Marlow, Associate Editor;
Brian Berding, Designer; Kellie McLaughlin, Chief Sales and
Marketing Officer; Richard Gregg, Sales Director, Books

Special thanks:
The Colors We Share was made possible, in part, with
generous support from Dawn and Chris Fleischner.

Aperture's programs are made possible, in part, by the New
York State Council on the Arts with the support of Governor
Andrew M. Cuomo and the New York State Legislature.

First edition, 2021
Printed in China
10 9 8 7 6 5 4 3 2 1

Library of Congress Cataloging-in-Publication Data

Names: Dass, Angélica, 1979- author, photographer.
Title: The colors we share / Angélica Dass.
Description: First edition. | New York, N.Y. : Aperture, 2021.
   | Audience:Ages 6-8. | Audience: Grades 2-3. |
   Summary: "Made for young readers, this book features
   portraits that celebrate the diverse beauty of human
   skin"--Provided by publisher.
Identifiers: LCCN 2021000425 | ISBN 9781597115018
   (hardcover)
Subjects: LCSH: Human skin color--Juvenile literature. |
   Multiculturalism--Juvenile literature. | Ethnology--Juvenile
   literature.
Classification: LCC GN197 .D37 2021 | DDC 612.7/927--dc23
LC record available at https://lccn.loc.gov/2021000425

To order Aperture books, or inquire about gift or
group orders, contact:
+1 212.946.7154
orders@aperture.org

For information about Aperture trade distribution
worldwide, visit:
aperture.org/distribution

aperture

Aperture Foundation
548 West 28th Street, 4th Floor
New York, NY 10001
aperture.org

Aperture, a not-for-profit foundation, connects the photo
community and its audiences with the most inspiring work,
the sharpest ideas, and with each other—in print, in person,
and online.

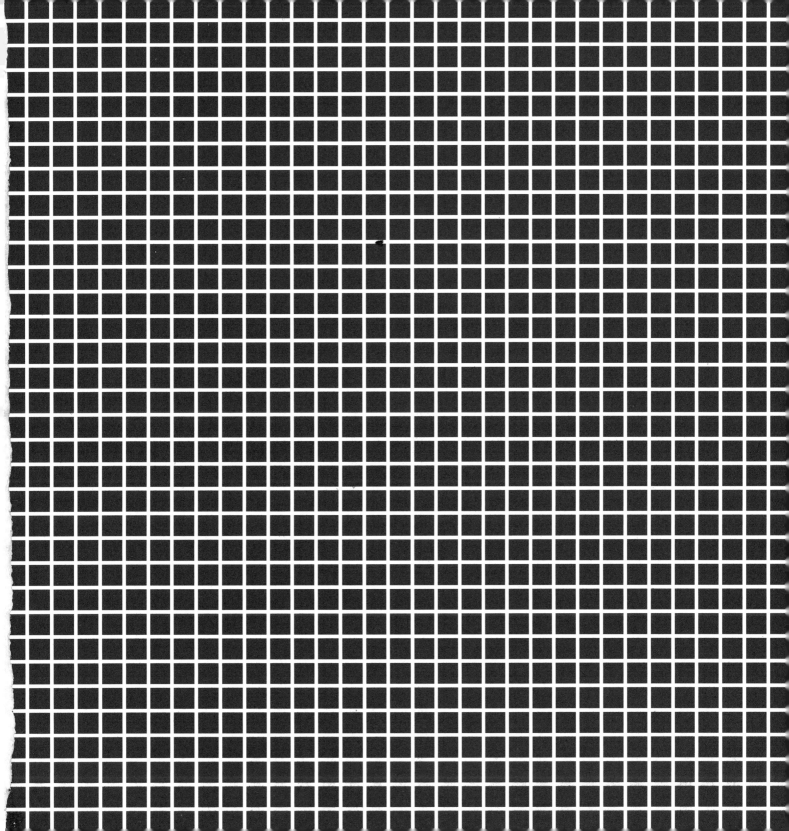